The]

(based

CW00920491

THE
SENIOR DEACON'S WORK
TODAY

by
G.F. Redman, P.G.Swd.B.,
Assistant Grand Secretary

(Member of the Committee of Emulation Lodge of
Improvement 1980–; Senior Member 2002–)

Lewis Masonic

Also by Graham Redman:

Cur non mitto meos tibi, Pontiliane, libellos?
Ne mihi tu mittas, Pontiliane, tuos.
Martial (A.D. 40-102)

Why don't I send you my little books, Pontilianus?
In case you send me yours!

First published 2011

ISBN 978 0 85318 388 4

Published by Lewis Masonic

an imprint of Ian Allan Publishing Ltd, Hersham, Surrey KT12 4RG.
Printed by Ian Allan Printing Ltd, Hersham, Surrey KT12 4RG

1109/A1

Visit the Lewis Masonic website at www.lewismasonic.com

Contents

Chapter 1

Introduction

This series of books sets out to provide for each Officer of a Lodge as accurate as possible a description of Emulation Working as it applies to his office. It is largely derived from my earlier book, *Emulation Working Today*, which does not slip conveniently into the pocket of a coat or apron, and it therefore aims to remedy that defect.

Each book in the series, like its bigger brother, *Emulation Working Today*, is intended as a *supplement* to the Emulation Ritual book. It does not claim to be exhaustive as a description of Emulation Working, for in many, if not most, cases the Emulation Ritual is quite clear as to the procedure that is to be followed. There are, however, many instances where, despite what might be thought a clear description in the rubric of the Ritual, Brethren commonly fail to carry out the action described in accordance with the practice of Emulation Lodge of Improvement (which, it should not be forgotten, preserves as far as possible the only Craft ritual that has ever been formally approved by the Grand Lodge). There can be various reasons for such failures: sometimes a weak or ignorant Director of Ceremonies or preceptor may have allowed Brethren to fall into careless habits; conversely a strong Director of Ceremonies or preceptor may have enforced his own idiosyncratic views; whichever may be the case, that fickle and shifting concept, the tradition of the Lodge, is usually invoked as justification. Leaving aside such shortcomings in the ritual actions, there are also several "accident black spots" where the wording of the ritual is liable regularly to be rendered inaccurately.

The books in this series therefore set out, first, to provide a second bearing where difficulties are known to arise, rather like the geometric principle which enables a surveyor or cartographer to pinpoint a spot by the process of triangulation. It is hoped that the additional and alternative descriptions provided in these books will render clearer those procedures which most often defeat Brethren. Secondly, by warning of the "black spots" and providing mnemonics or other strategies to help pass through them safely, this series is aimed at making the task of the various Officers of a Lodge easier. Finally, I have included two short appendices, the first containing a checklist and the second covering techniques for memorising and remembering the ritual.

Few authors can resist the temptation at times to present their own private opinions to their readers, and I do not claim to be an exception to the general rule. I have tried, however, as far as practicable, to keep the books in this series factual and descriptive, even though I have found it impossible to avoid occasionally expressing my own views on matters that some might regard as mildly controversial.

As a final observation, and rather an obvious one, the greater amount of detail now shown in the rubrics of the ritual has undoubtedly encouraged Brethren in the view that there is no longer any need to attend a Lodge of Instruction in order to learn the correct method of working. While it is eminently possible – and it is, indeed, the easiest way – to learn the words of the ritual from a book, the actions are a different matter. For them there is ultimately no substitute for the kind of experience to be gained in a Lodge of Instruction. This book will take a Brother part – perhaps even most – of the way but it is not the same as receiving instruction at first hand from a competent preceptor or attending a Lodge of demonstration such as Emulation Lodge of Improvement.

Chapter 2

General Remarks

Succeeding chapters in this book deal with the specific duties of the Senior Deacon. But of course every Brother has a certain minimum of ritual actions to perform, even if it is only to stand to order during the opening and closing of the Lodge. Similarly, certain actions are common to all the Officers of a Lodge. This chapter, therefore, deals with those basic matters.

There is no matter more basic than that of the signs in the three degrees. Signs are given when the Master or some other Officer directs; during the obligations; and when addressing a superior Officer. At no time during the ceremonies as carried out in Emulation Lodge of Improvement does an Officer stand to order when an exchange is *originated* by the Master or a superior Officer. The best illustration of this point is the ceremony of opening the Lodge in the second or third degree. When the Junior Warden addresses the Inner Guard, the latter does not stand to order. But a few moments later when he reports back to his superior, he does take a step and give the sign, because it is he who is initiating the exchange.

In almost every case, a necessary preliminary to the giving of a sign is the taking of a step. The notable exception to this is the sign of R. given during prayers, when a step is not necessary. Some have even claimed that this is not strictly a sign at all, but an *attitude* of R.; it is certainly the case that it is not the sign of any degree. Otherwise, the only exception to the general rule is in the Traditional History of the third degree when the first two signs are demonstrated in the course of the narrative.

In Emulation Working, all the signs of the three degrees are given with the hand open throughout. The practice, commonly met with, of closing the fist as the sign is discharged is firmly discouraged as being slovenly, though to many it may appear stylish. Signs are also given silently, except when greeting the newly installed Master during the ceremony of Installation. In fact, the general rule is that all signs should be given quietly and smartly, but without any undue ostentation.

The correct method of giving all the signs is fully detailed in the text and rubric of the Emulation Ritual, but it may be helpful to reinforce the following points. First, in Emulation Working the sign of the first degree does not start by placing the hand straight out in front of the body; the hand is brought immediately to the position in which the sign is held. Secondly, the sign of R. differs from the sign of F. in that the thumb lies parallel to, or even concealed by, the fingers, and is discharged by being dropped rather than cut. (It is sometimes debated whether it is the sign of F. or the sign of R. that should be given at the end of the closing, to accompany the words, "F., F., F.". It should be neither: the Lodge is by then closed and therefore any sign is inappropriate; the Brethren merely make a threefold gesture with the r.h. on the l.b..) Thirdly, the first sign of a Master Mason is given in two distinct movements, the first of which is to the front and *not* to the side, still less to the rear: the d. and a.s. is assumed to be directly in front. Fourthly, the p...l sign of a Master Mason is given in different ways according to whether it is to be held or to be immediately discharged. In the former case the hand is brought initially to the centre where it is held (in Emulation Working the sign is not first given to the point of recovery and then held); when the sign is to be discharged the hand is then carried first to the opposite side. If the sign is to be immediately discharged, for example in opening the Lodge in the third degree or when the Master Masons pass round the Lodge and salute the newly-installed Master, the hand is brought immediately direct to the opposite side, without even a momentary pause at the centre. In every case the person giving the sign recovers at the end, except at the moment of opening in the third degree, when recovery is unnecessary, since it has already taken place a minute or two earlier. Finally, when the G. or R. sign is given audibly as a greeting in the Installation ceremony, the first movement is upwards and the sign does *not* begin with a slap of the thighs; when the sign is given silently, the tips of the fingers should touch at the top.

In Emulation Working, during an obligation, the Brethren stand to order with the p...l sign; the sign of F. is used only in the second degree, not, as in the case of some other workings, whenever an obligation is taken. The sign is discharged as soon as the Candidate has finished repeating the words of the obligation, and before he seals it. In this respect also Emulation differs from many other workings, as well as certain other degrees beyond the Craft. Whilst, however, there may be an argument for holding the sign of F. until the Candidate has sealed, it is difficult to see any obvious reason why a *p...l* sign should be held beyond the end of the obligation itself.

The sign of the degree is always given when entering or retiring from the Lodge, except during the ceremony of Installation when Entered Apprentices, Fellow Crafts and Master Masons retire and later re-enter together. A Brother entering the Lodge for the first time during a meeting gives the signs of every degree in which the Lodge has been opened; if he wishes to extend his apologies for his late arrival he does so while holding the sign of the highest degree. A Brother retiring from the Lodge or returning to it, gives only the sign of the degree in which the Lodge is then open. The only exception to this is a Candidate for passing or raising, who gives, under the direction of the Deacon, all the signs of the degrees up to and including the one in which the Lodge is then open.

When the Brethren stand together as part of the ritual they should do so, taking their cue in this – as in many other instances – from the Master, only *after* the Junior Warden has knocked, and not as soon as the Master has done so.

In Emulation Working, the words "So mote it be" are spoken by the Immediate Past Master (*i.e.* the preceptor) alone. In most Private Lodges, however, they are said or sung by all the Brethren present.

In the first degree, when the Candidate is restored to light, the Brethren should be careful to synchronise their handclap with the descent of the Master's gavel. Similarly at a later stage when the Senior Warden invests the Candidate.

Towards the end of the explanation of the second degree Tracing Board the sign of R. is given only *after* the words "denoting G." and *not* as soon as the Brethren stand.

During the ceremony of Installation, when the Master Masons, Fellow Crafts and Entered Apprentices perambulate the Lodge, each pauses briefly before the Master's pedestal and, still facing south, gives the sign by way of salute to the newly-installed Master. In Emulation, these signs are not given "in passing", and the Lodge is squared. (I should, however, add that in many other workings the signs are given in passing, and that that is the case under the direction of the Grand Director of Ceremonies or one of his Deputies when a Consecration or Installation is carried out by a senior Grand Officer.)

There is sometimes confusion as to whether a Brother standing in for one of the Officers should wear the collar and jewel of that office. The answer is set out clearly in the booklet *Information for the Guidance of Members of the Craft*. If the particular Officer is present, he alone may wear the collar, and a Brother temporarily performing his duties for him does not wear it. But if the Officer is absent, the stand-in should wear it.

Another matter where there is uncertainty among many members of the Craft is in relation to the use of the prefix "Worshipful". In Emulation, the only person addressed as "Worshipful" is the Master; and he should *always* be addressed as "Worshipful Master" – never as just "Master". No one else is so addressed, or even referred to, either by name or by reference to his Office. Thus "Worshipful Brother Secretary" is contrary to the practice of Emulation Lodge of Improvement, and it is suggested that as a matter of principle it is wrong, since the prefix "Worshipful", except in the case of the Master, belongs to the *individual* and not to the *Office*.

Whilst it cannot be said that to address or refer to someone as "Worshipful Brother Smith" is wrong, there is no doubt in my mind that it is unnecessary. Even less desirable, however, is the uneasy mixture of the formal and the informal, more commonly met with at dinner than in the Lodge, represented by the prefix "Worshipful" with a Brother's first name alone. "Brother Smith" is correct Emulation Working – and quite sufficient; "Worshipful Brother Smith" is acceptable, as in some cases is "Brother John"; but "Worshipful Brother John" is neither one thing nor the other and really will not do.

It is sometimes said that no ritual or ceremonial practice in Masonry is actually wrong. Clearly this cannot be true; some things *are* wrong. But what the proponents of this view mean is that there are wide tolerances as to what is permissible. No Brother should forget this, particularly when visiting a Lodge which uses a different working from that with which he is familiar. We are all prone to assume that the way that we do things in our own Lodge is the only – or at any rate the best – way. But just because a Lodge does something differently, we should not be hasty to condemn it as wrong.

Chapter 3

The Office of Senior Deacon

This is the third of the "progressive" offices with ritual duties. Those duties are more extensive than those of the Junior Deacon, in that the Senior Deacon has charge of the Candidate in two ceremonies, but they are not more important or more demanding.

The Deacons' duties fall into two categories – the ritual and the procedural. Ironically, it is only the latter which are mentioned at the opening of the Lodge (perhaps because the original meaning of "deacon" is "messenger" or "servant"), but the former, which are drawn to the attention of each of the Deacons on his investiture, are much the more important.

In Emulation Lodge of Improvement the Senior Deacon has no duties to perform during the ceremonies of opening and closing the Lodge in the three degrees.

The Senior Deacon should ensure that he is thoroughly familiar with the general matters dealt with in the last chapter, as well as the specific duties which are described below. In Emulation Lodge of Improvement the Senior Deacon sits in his old position, on the immediate right of the Master, directly facing the Inner Guard. In most regular Lodges, however, the

Senior Deacon sits at the extreme eastern end of the front row of seats on the north side of the Lodge. He carries a wand as his badge of office, but only during the performance of his ritual duties in the ceremonies of Initiation, Passing and Raising. When he carries it, he should always do so with dignity. While he is on the move, the butt of the wand should be a few inches above the floor, and when he is at rest the butt should rest on the floor of the Lodge. On no account should a Deacon lean upon his wand for support; nor should he carry it other than in his right hand – and in an upright position – except where the ritual specifically requires him to do so.

There is no single correct method of holding the wand; some Deacons hold it in the lightly clenched fist with the forearm parallel to the ground; but the better method is for the Deacon to hold it lightly in the crook of the hand between the thumb and forefinger, using the remaining fingers of the right hand to steady it, at the point where the hand naturally grasps it if the elbow is very slightly bent and the butt of the wand is resting on the ground. If the wand is supported in this manner, then by bending the elbow so that his forearm is at an angle of forty-five degrees to the horizontal the Deacon can lift his wand to the optimum position for carrying it while he is on the move.

In general the Senior Deacon takes hold of the Candidate only when he leads him from one part of the Lodge to another. As the Notes on Ritual and Procedure in the front of the Emulation Ritual point out, the manner of holding the Candidate is a matter of common sense, and not of ritual. The Junior Deacon should adopt whatever method gives him the greatest degree of control, having regard to the relative heights of himself and the Candidate. It is, however, almost invariably the case that the Deacon will find it easier to manage the Candidate if his left arm is behind the Candidate's right arm, than if it is in front.

The Senior Deacon should be careful to distinguish between those directions and prompts to the Candidate which are printed in black in the Emulation Ritual and those which are merely contained within the rubric. The former are always given aloud, so that they can be heard by all in the Lodge; the latter should only be given in a whisper or a low voice as they do not form a part of the ritual wording.

All instructions in the course of a perambulation, except for directions to the Candidate to salute or advance to one of the principal Officers, are given in a whisper or a low voice. During perambulations, and only during perambulations, the Lodge is squared. On all other occasions the Senior Deacon leads the

Candidate by the shortest route (*i.e.* in a straight line). When squaring is to be carried out, the Senior Deacon and the Candidate halt, turn right, make a momentary pause, and then step off together with the left foot. In the second degree, the Candidate is the pivot; that is to say, the Senior Deacon wheels backwards, while the Candidate turns on his own ground. In the third degree, however, the Senior Deacon must be the pivot so as to allow the Junior Deacon, who is close behind the Candidate, room to square the Lodge before all three step off again together.

I have already stated that in Emulation Lodge of Improvement the Deacons carry their wands only when performing their ritual duties in the ceremonies of the three degrees. Their procedural duties generally involve fetching and carrying, and in the execution of these a wand is an embarrassment.

For the Senior Deacon the first of these duties relates to the Minutes. In Emulation Lodge of Improvement, the Minutes are not signed by the Master. In a regular Lodge, however, it is the duty of the Senior Deacon to carry the Minute Book to the Master for signature. On no account should he rest the Minute Book on the V.S.L. while the Master signs.

Another, and perhaps the most important, of these duties is the conducting of ballots. In Emulation Lodge of Improvement, while the Junior Deacon distributes the tokens the Senior Deacon takes the ballot box to the south side of the Master's pedestal, where he stands square, facing north, so that the ballot box may be checked. He then collects the tokens starting with the Immediate Past Master, and finishing with the Master, whose token he collects at the north side of his pedestal. He then proceeds to the south side, where he again stands square, facing north, until the result of the ballot has been declared. He then replaces the ballot box on the Secretary's table, returns to his place and sits.

In Emulation Lodge of Improvement there is no occasion for a "paper" ballot, but the above method will do equally well for such a purpose. Some Masons hold that the Master, as the most important person in the Lodge, should be the first to receive a token or paper, and the first to cast his vote. The Emulation practice is, however, that given above, and may easily be justified by an appeal to the very same principle, on the basis that the progression is an upward one, by way of the Junior Warden, then the Senior, through the Grand Officers to the Master.

In Emulation Lodge of Improvement, it is also part of the Deacons' duties to collect the dues at each meeting. The Senior Deacon starts with the Immediate

Past Master and finishes with the Senior Warden. The Junior Deacon starts with the Inner Guard and finishes with the Master. Each takes his bag straight to the Secretary's table as soon as he has finished his collection.

Chapter 4

The First Degree

In the ceremony of Initiation the Senior Deacon has few duties, and they are relatively straightforward. He should, however, note the following points.

After the Master has ordered the admission of the Candidate and called on the Deacons, the Senior Deacon makes his way with his wand to the north of the Senior Warden's pedestal, places the kneeling stool (preferably by drawing it along the floor, whilst keeping his wand *upright*) and takes up a position on the right of the Junior Deacon. The Senior Deacon should be careful, if the stool is slightly angled, rather than flat, to check that it is angled in the correct direction so that the Candidate can kneel comfortably. The Deacons should always endeavour to ensure that they set off to the door simultaneously with the Inner Guard; if properly carried out this small procession can be very impressive The Senior Deacon is on the right, so that when the procession reaches the door and the Deacons turn about he will be to the left of the Candidate. When the Candidate has been admitted, the Senior Deacon accompanies him and the Junior Deacon to the kneeling stool, and halts.

When the Master gavels for the prayer, each Deacon transfers his wand to his left hand to cross it above the Candidate's head, and gives the sign of R. with his right. It is quite immaterial, in Emulation Working, whether the Junior Deacon's wand is crossed in front of the Senior Deacon's, or *vice versa*.

After the prayer and the further examination of the Candidate by the Master, it is the Senior Deacon's duty to draw the kneeling stool aside once the Candidate has risen. He replaces it in front of the Senior Warden's pedestal as soon as the Junior Deacon and the Candidate have started their perambulation. The Senior Deacon then takes the p....d from the Senior Warden's pedestal, where it has been placed by the Inner Guard, and carries it to the Master's pedestal. He places it directly on to the Master's pedestal and does not hand it to the Master himself. He then returns to his place and sits.

Before the Obligation, the Senior Deacon should take care to time his arrival at the Master's pedestal so that it coincides with that of the Junior Deacon and the Candidate. At the appropriate point he must not forget to raise the Candidate's left hand so that the Master may position the Cs. in it; similarly, at the end of the Obligation he must be ready to assist in lowering the Candidate's left hand after the Master has removed the

Cs. When the Master gavels for the Obligation both Deacons give the sign, not forgetting to take a step, and hold their wands in their left hands, crossed over the Candidate's head, as at the prayer. Again it is immaterial which wand is in front of the other. They lower their wands when the sign is discharged, that is, immediately after the Candidate has repeated the final words of the Obligation and *before* he seals it on the V.S.L..

As soon as the Candidate has been raised after the Obligation, the Senior Deacon makes a left turn, returns to his place and sits. He has no further duties during the ceremony.

Chapter 5

The Second Degree

The Senior Deacon plays no part in the questioning and subsequent entrustment with the p.g. and p.w. that takes place while the Lodge is in the first degree. During the actual ceremony of Passing, however, the Senior Deacon has charge of the Candidate from the time that the latter is admitted. It may be helpful to him to note that when a prayer is about to be delivered after a Candidate has re-entered the Lodge, he is directed to *advance*; on other occasions he is directed (as on retiring) to *salute* the Worshipful Master.

After the Master has ordered the admission of the Candidate and called on the Deacons, the Senior Deacon makes his way with his wand to the north of the Senior Warden's pedestal, where the Junior Deacon will have placed the kneeling stool and have taken up a position to his right. The Deacons should always endeavour to ensure that they set off to the door simultaneously with the Inner Guard. It should be noted that on the way to the door the Senior Deacon is on the left, so that when the procession reaches the door and the Deacons turn about he will be to the right of the Candidate. When the Inner Guard steps aside after elevating the Sq., the Senior Deacon takes the Candidate firmly by the right hand, whispers instructions, leads him to the kneeling stool, and halts. When the Candidate is directed to kneel, the Deacon whispers such instructions as are necessary, and ensures that the Candidate gives the sign of R., adjusting his thumb if necessary. When the Master gavels for the prayer, each Deacon transfers his wand to his left hand to cross it above the Candidate's head, and gives the sign of R. with his right. It is quite immaterial, in Emulation Working, whether the Junior Deacon's wand is crossed in front of the Senior Deacon's, or *vice versa*. After the prayer, the Senior Deacon checks that the Candidate drops the sign of R., whispering instructions if necessary.

After the recital of the prayer, the Candidate is conducted twice round the Lodge – once to prove himself in the first degree and once to show himself as the Candidate for the second. The two perambulations follow the pattern described in Chapter 3 and should present no difficulty. The Senior Deacon should, however, be careful that the Candidate, when he halts on the floor of the Lodge level with the Master's or a Warden's pedestal and is directed to salute, does not turn his head or body towards the Officer being saluted, but continues to face to the front. Moreover, in Emulation Working the Deacon does *not* take a step and give the sign with the Candidate.

When the halt is made at the east side of the Junior Warden's pedestal it should be noted that in Emulation Lodge of Improvement (and most regular Lodges) the layout of the Lodge Room is such that to lead the Candidate to the side of the Junior Warden's pedestal, the Deacon has to carry out a "sideways shuffle" to the left, reversing the procedure in order to regain the floor of the Lodge after the examination. It should also be noted that when at the side of the Wardens' pedestals the Senior Deacon and Candidate should stand square (*i.e.* facing west at the Junior Warden's, and north at the Senior Warden's pedestal) and the Deacon should turn only his head to address the Warden. At the conclusion of the colloquy, the Deacon and Candidate regain the floor of the Lodge, normally by a "sideways shuffle" to the right (*i.e.* reversing the earlier procedure). If, however, space permits, there can be no objection to this manoeuvre being carried out by a "double wheeling" movement; that is, by the Deacon wheeling backwards using the Candidate as a pivot, as during squaring, and then stepping off, describing a wider wheel, to bring the Candidate back on to the floor of the Lodge.

When, during the second perambulation, the Lodge

is to be squared immediately before conducting the Candidate to the south side of the Senior Warden's pedestal, it is important that the Senior Deacon continues in a westerly direction, stepping off the carpet if necessary, until he and the Candidate are level with (*i.e.* due south of) the side of the pedestal. The Lodge is then squared in the normal fashion. It should be noted in this connection that even if the Lodge Room is very narrow, at least one step must be taken by the Deacon and Candidate after the turn, in order to complete the action of squaring.

When the Candidate has to be conducted from the south to the north side of the Senior Warden's pedestal, this may be carried out either by a "sideways shuffle" on to the floor of the Lodge, followed by a wheeling movement, or by the Deacon, if he feels sufficiently confident, wheeling the Candidate backwards so that he faces east, and then describing a semi-circular wheel from one side of the pedestal to the other. Whichever method is adopted, this particular manoeuvre is followed by the Senior Deacon placing the Candidate's hand in that of the Senior Warden. After doing so, he takes up a position on the Candidate's left, and ensures that the latter is facing east.

After the Master has replied to the Warden's presentation, the Senior Deacon must be ready to receive the Candidate's hand back from the Senior Warden, and to take up a position on the Candidate's right. In effect the Candidate and Deacon simply change places at this juncture; there is no need at all for the Senior Deacon to lead the Candidate forward to the edge of the carpet.

When directed by the Senior Warden to instruct the Candidate to advance to the east, the Senior Deacon leads him to a point on the north side of the Lodge opposite the imaginary foot of the w.s., turns him to face south and moves to the centre-line of the Lodge.

If there is one procedure in Emulation Working which more than any other is consistently carried out incorrectly in Private Lodges, it is the method of advancing from west to east in this degree. The first – and essential – point which the Senior Deacon must grasp is that the imaginary w.s. runs in a semi-circle from a point on the *centre-line* of the Lodge about two yards short of the Master's pedestal to a point on the *centre-line* of the Lodge directly in front of the pedestal. It does not, despite the illustration shown on most Tracing Boards (including that used in Emulation Lodge of Improvement), take the form of a quarter circle starting on the north side of the Lodge and ending directly in front of the Master's pedestal, but that is a mistake very commonly made. The second point is that the Candidate must arrive at the pedestal with his feet together in the form of a square, left foot pointing north and right foot pointing east, so that he is able to kneel, without further movement, in the proper attitude. The correct method of performing the manoeuvre is as follows.

Having positioned the Candidate on the north side of the Lodge facing south, the Senior Deacon proceeds, as already mentioned, to the foot of the imaginary w.s., where he briefly addresses the Candidate. He then turns about, and immediately places his feet in the form of a square, left foot pointing south and right foot pointing west. He steps off with the left foot, which he places pointing due south. The second step, with the right foot, is taken in a south-easterly direction; the third, with the left foot, is taken due east; the fourth, with the right foot, north-east; and the fifth step, with the left foot, is taken to a point immediately in front of the pedestal, that foot pointing north, and the right foot being brought in a closing motion heel to heel with the left in the form of a square. Note the following points:-

(a) Each step is taken at forty-five degrees to the preceding one.

(b) At each step the foot must be raised rather higher than in the ordinary course of walking, to signify the upward direction of the w.s.. This movement should not, however, be exaggerated; a little short of knee-height is quite sufficient.

(c) The Senior Deacon does *not* give a running commentary on the procedure.

The Senior Deacon, having reached the pedestal, then turns right, and following the line of the w.s. in the reverse direction, but with an ordinary walking motion and without slavishly following the precise position of the individual steps, makes his way back to the Candidate He takes him by the right hand and leads or draws him to the foot of the w.s., directing him to place his feet in the form of a square. He then releases his hand. In this degree, unlike the former, the Deacon does not tell the Candidate first to place his feet together and then turn the right one out; instead he ensures that he comes *straight into* the starting position. All instructions for this and the succeeding procedure are given in a whisper or low voice. The Senior Deacon does not hold the Candidate's hand when he advances up the w.s., but directs him by standing a little in front of and facing him, and indicating with the butt of his wand the correct position for the next step. When the Candidate arrives at the pedestal, he takes up a position on his right.

When the Candidate is asked if he is willing to take the Obligation, the Senior Deacon must *not* prompt him to answer in the affirmative; if the Candidate hesitates for more than a moment or two the Deacon should whisper "Answer", but the choice must the Candidate's own. Before the Obligation he receives the Sq. from the Immediate Past Master at the appropriate moment and passes it, behind the Candidate, to the Junior Deacon. When the Master gavels for the Obligation the Senior Deacon gives the sign, not forgetting to take a step, and both Deacons hold their wands in their left hands, crossed over the Candidate's head, as at the prayer. Again it is immaterial which wand is in front of the other. The Deacons lower their wands when the sign is discharged, that is, immediately after the Candidate has repeated the final words of the Obligation and *before* he seals it on the V.S.L.. At the end of the Obligation, the Senior Deacon receives the Sq. back from the Junior Deacon and returns it to the Immediate Past Master. When the Candidate is directed to seal his Obligation, the Deacon should not apply pressure to the back of his head unless the Candidate hesitates, and then only gentle pressure should be used – by way of indication rather than by way of force.

Once the Candidate has been raised by the Master, the Senior Deacon leads him to the north side of the Master's pedestal, taking care that there is sufficient room for the Candidate to take two short steps. During the entrustment which follows, the Candidate is in the charge of the Master. The Senior Deacon should therefore only intervene if it is absolutely necessary. (The Deacon does not take a step or give the signs with the Candidate.) When he comes to dictate to the Candidate the answers he is to give in the colloquy with the Master, it is essential that he is exceedingly quick off the mark in giving the prompt for the answer to the third question, in order to ensure that the Candidate does not speak the word.

During the perambulation which follows, the Lodge is squared as before (and when approaching the Senior Warden's pedestal, in the same manner as in the second of the earlier perambulations). When the Deacon addresses the Wardens with step and sign, he does not transfer his wand to the left hand. The correct method is for him to rest the butt of the wand on the floor and the top of it in the crook of his right shoulder. Depending on the nature of the floor covering at the particular spot, he may find it necessary to lodge the butt of the wand against the foot of the pedestal or the candlestick to prevent it from slipping. Just as at the Master's pedestal a minute or two earlier, the Deacon does not take the step or give the sign with the Candidate. After he has placed the Candidate's hand in that of the Warden for the communication of the Tn., he adjusts the Candidate's thumb *from above*. He must always ensure that the phrases in which he dictates the responses to the Candidate are of a sensible length, which the Candidate will have no difficulty in repeating. It is of particular importance that at the Senior Warden's pedestal, after the Candidate has advanced as an E.A., the Deacon whispers to him next to take the step only, and he must be ready, if necessary, to lay a gentle restraining hand on the Candidate's arm. It is also important that when the Candidate explains to what the p...l sign alludes, the Deacon dictates the answer in the correct tense – "would rather *have had* his ...." – and that he ensures that the Candidate synchronises his action with the words.

The Candidate is conducted from the south to the north side of the Senior Warden's pedestal in the same manner as in the second of the earlier perambulations.

When the Candidate is invested with the badge of the degree, the Senior Deacon may assist the Senior

Warden, if necessary, during the act of clothing, but he must stand facing east when the Senior Warden addresses the Candidate. As the Senior Warden sits, the Deacon receives the Candidate's hand from him and takes up a position between the Warden and the Candidate, both of them facing east; it is not necessary to advance to the edge of the carpet.

When he is directed by the Master to place the Candidate at the south-east part of the Lodge, the Senior Deacon leads him *via* the north and east, squaring the Lodge. This might appear to be an exception to the general rule that the Lodge is squared only in the course of a perambulation, but in truth, this particular movement should be regarded as the continuation of the perambulation. The Senior Deacon should note that as the Lodge has to be squared at the south-east corner, it is essential that he and the Candidate take at least one step along the south side of the Lodge to complete the process, before he wheels backwards so that he and the Candidate are facing north.

When the Senior Deacon conducts the Candidate to the Master's pedestal for the explanation of the W.Ts., this should be done in a wide wheeling movement.

When the Candidate retires to restore his comfort, the Senior Deacon wheels him forwards (anti-clockwise) at the Master's pedestal, leads him direct to the north of the Senior Warden's pedestal, wheels backwards (clockwise), and directs him to salute. After the Candidate has done so, he then wheels with him forwards again and leads him to the door of the Lodge, endeavouring to synchronise the latter movement with the Inner Guard. (This procedure illustrates two basic principles: first, that when the Candidate has to execute an about-turn from east to west, or *vice versa*, the Senior Deacon should always keep himself between the Candidate and the Master's pedestal; and secondly that, as has already been mentioned, except during a perambulation, the Lodge is not squared, but the shortest route is taken.)

The procedure during the remainder of the ceremony presents little difficulty. As soon as the Inner Guard has been told by the Master to admit the Candidate on the latter's return, the Senior Deacon stands and makes his way to the door, preceded by the Inner Guard. He leads the Candidate to the edge of the carpet, and directs him to salute the Master. Once the Candidate has saluted, the Senior Deacon leads him direct to the foot of the Tracing Board for the Explanation. At the conclusion of the Explanation, he must not forget to take the Candidate to a seat in the Lodge. No particular place is prescribed in Emulation Working. Some might argue that just as the Initiate is given a seat in the north-east part of the Lodge, the Candidate who has just been passed should be accommodated in the south-east part. This is not, however, a matter of ritual, and Lodges may follow their own inclination.

Chapter 6

The Third Degree

In the ceremony of Raising, the Senior Deacon has charge of the Candidate throughout, except when he is under the direction of the Master and his Wardens. During the questions before Raising it is his duty to prompt the Candidate in his answers if it should prove necessary; he must therefore ensure that he is familiar with the answers himself. Once the Candidate has answered the questions, the Deacon conducts him direct to the north of the Master's pedestal for entrustment. After the Candidate has been entrusted with the p.g. and p.w. by the Master, the Senior Deacon leads him direct to the north of the Senior Warden's pedestal, wheels him backwards, directs him to salute, then, after he has done so, wheels him forwards and leads him, in step with the Inner Guard, to the door of the Lodge.

As soon as the Lodge has been opened or resumed in the third degree, the Deacons lay out the s...t. In Emulation Working the s...t is always laid fully open, and it is the responsibility of the Senior Deacon to select the correct distance from the front of the Master's pedestal. If he takes four good paces diagonally from his place to the mid-line of the Lodge, he should find that the point at which he arrives is the right place for the eastern edge of the s...t (not the eastern edge of the g...e), and he should not move from that point, but should wait for the Junior Deacon to bring the s...t to him. The method of spreading the s...t is a matter of common sense, but it is astonishing how frequently it is done in an untidy or unmethodical fashion. The best method of carrying out the procedure is as follows.

The s...t will normally have been folded in three lengthways, parallel to the centre-line of the g...e, and then folded or rolled in the other direction. The s...t should, if possible, be unfolded or unrolled only in the one direction, and not fully opened, before being laid (correctly orientated, and still folded in three) on the floor. Once the central portion of the s...t is in position, the sides can be spread. Each Deacon places a foot as an anchor at the centre point of his end (if one Deacon uses his right foot, the other must use his left), then taking the uppermost corner of the s...t in his opposite hand carries that hand and the corresponding foot away from the centre of the s...t, thus spreading one side. He then brings that foot back to the centre, places it on the s...t to keep it anchored, and repeats the process with the other hand and foot, thus spreading the other side. The correct and co-ordinated use of this method will ensure that the s...t is laid swiftly and smoothly, and without any significant creases. It also looks extremely stylish. A broadly similar procedure in reverse is followed to refold the s...t, though the foot is placed a third of the way along the end of the s...t in order to make each fold and it may be necessary to change hands in the act of folding.

After the Master has ordered the admission of the Candidate and called on the Deacons, the Senior Deacon makes his way with his wand to the north of the Senior Warden's pedestal, where the Junior Deacon will have placed the kneeling stool and have taken up a position to his right. The Deacons should always endeavour to ensure that they set off to the door simultaneously with the Inner Guard. It should be noted that on the way to the door the Senior Deacon is on the left, so that when the procession reaches the door and the Deacons turn about he will be to the right of the Candidate. When the Inner Guard steps aside after elevating the Cs., the Senior Deacon takes the Candidate firmly by the right hand, whispers instructions, leads him to the kneeling stool, and halts. When the Candidate is directed to kneel, the Deacon whispers such instructions as are necessary, and ensures that the Candidate gives the sign of R., adjusting his thumb if necessary. When the Master gavels for the prayer, each Deacon transfers his wand to his left hand to cross it above the Candidate's head, and gives the sign of R. with his right. It is immaterial, in Emulation Working, whether the Junior Deacon's wand is crossed in front of the Senior Deacon's, or *vice versa*. After the prayer, the Senior Deacon checks that the Candidate drops the sign of R., whispering instructions if necessary.

After the recital of the prayer, the Candidate is conducted three times round the Lodge – once to prove himself in the first degree, once to prove himself in the second and once to show himself as the Candidate for the third. The three perambulations are conducted in the same way as those in the second degree (see Chapter 5), except that:

(a) when the Lodge is squared in this degree the Senior Deacon must be the pivot so as to allow the Junior Deacon, who is close behind the Candidate, room to square the Lodge before all three step off again together; and

(b) in regaining the floor of the Lodge after an examination by one of the Wardens a "sideways shuffle" must always be used.

In addition, the Senior Deacon will need to leave room

for the Junior Deacon to take up a position on the Candidate's left when a halt is made at the end of the second perambulation. Otherwise the ceremony calls for no comment down to the time when the Senior Warden directs the Deacons to instruct the Candidate to advance to the east.

This is another procedure which is rarely carried out correctly. The Senior Deacon conducts the Candidate, followed by the Junior Deacon, to a point on the north side of the Lodge level with the centre of the s...t. He wheels the Candidate to face south, releases his hand and proceeds to a point half way along the south side of the s...t (without stepping on the latter if he can avoid it), where he briefly addresses the Candidate. He then goes straight to the head of the g...e, and immediately places his feet in the form of a square, left foot pointing east and right foot pointing south. He steps off with the left foot, which he places pointing due north about *a third* of the way along the north edge of the g...e, rapidly bringing up his right foot in the form of a square. The second step, starting with the right foot, is taken to a point *two-thirds* of the way along the south edge of the g...e, rapidly closing with the left foot as before, so that the right foot points south and the left east. The third step, starting with the left foot, is taken to the foot of the g...e, rapidly closing with the right foot, so that the left foot points east and the right south. The procedure is completed by four ordinary paces, starting with the left foot, not forgetting to close the fourth step with the left foot, so as to bring the heels together. Note the following points:-

(a) The first three steps are awkward, and it is vital that momentum is maintained by bringing the hind foot up to the leading foot *rapidly*. This comment applies with at least equal force when the Candidate comes to advance a few moments later. If either Senior Deacon or Candidate pauses with his feet straddling the g...e, the manoeuvre is not only rendered extremely difficult, if not impossible, but looks more than faintly ridiculous.

(b) The first two steps present a special difficulty in that the leading foot finishes pointing in a direction diametrically opposite to that from which the hind foot starts. Apart from maintaining the momentum, as already urged, the Deacon will find it easiest if in each case he rests the heel of the leading foot on the finishing point, but with the toes pointing east, and pivots on his heel into the correct position as he closes with the hind foot. In practice, it is a counsel of perfection to expect a Candidate (particularly as the Lodge is in darkness) to orientate his feet correctly after the first and second steps, and the Senior Deacon should be content if the Candidate's feet are the correct distance along the g...e.

(c) The third step is frequently rendered more difficult by the Senior Deacon or the Candidate not moving far enough along the g...e at the first and second steps. If the points mentioned at (a) and (b) are observed, both Deacon and Candidate should be able to achieve a greater forward advance on the first two steps.

(d) The Senior Deacon does not deliver a running commentary as he carries out the procedure.

The Senior Deacon returns to the Candidate *via* the south side of the s...t, taking care not to step on the g....e. He takes him by the right hand and leads or draws him to the head of the g...e, directing him to place his feet in the form of a square. He then releases his hand. In this degree, as in the second, the Deacon does not tell the Candidate first to place his feet together and then turn the right one out; instead he ensures that he comes *straight into* the starting position. All instructions for this and the succeeding procedure are given in a whisper or low voice. The Senior Deacon does not hold the Candidate's hand when he advances along the g...e, but directs him by standing on the south side of the g...e, a little ahead of the Candidate, and indicating with the butt of his wand the correct position for the next step. Similarly, he does not hold the Candidate's hand during the last four steps, but walks beside him to the pedestal, where he takes up a position on his right.

When the Candidate is asked if he is willing to take the Obligation, the Senior Deacon must *not* prompt him to answer in the affirmative; if the Candidate hesitates for more than a moment or two the Deacon should whisper "Answer", but the choice must the Candidate's own. When the Master gavels for the Obligation both Deacons give the sign, not forgetting to take a step, and hold their wands in their left hands, crossed over the Candidate's head, as at the prayer. (Again it is immaterial which wand is in front of the other.) They lower their wands when the sign is discharged, that is, immediately after the Candidate has repeated the final words of the

Obligation and *before* he seals it on the V.S.L..

Once the Master has raised the Candidate after the Obligation and resumed his seat, the Deacons back the Candidate between them to the foot of the g....e. This means that all three will normally be standing on the s...t, though the Candidate must not be on the g...e itself. The Deacons do not hold the Candidate's hands. When the Wardens are summoned by the Master at the end of the Exhortation, the Senior Deacon stands fast until he is tapped on his left shoulder by the Junior Warden. He then takes one pace sideways to his right to enable the Warden to stand between him and the Candidate. The line of five thus formed is held for a moment, and then the Senior Deacon turns right (simultaneously with the Junior Deacon turning left) and returns behind the Wardens and Candidate to his place, taking care not to step on the g....e, and sits.

When the Master concludes the communication of the secrets, the Senior Deacon rises and goes straight to the right of the Candidate, taking care not to cross the path of the Master as the latter returns to the Chair. He takes him by the right hand and leads him to the north of the Senior Warden's pedestal, where he instructs him to salute the Master, remembering to give him the direction "P...l sign only in the third" in a low voice or a whisper.

On the Candidate's return, the direction "Full signs"

is similarly given *sotto voce*. The Senior Deacon then takes the Candidate by the right hand and draws him backwards to the Senior Warden to be presented for investiture; the Senior Deacon may assist the Senior Warden, if necessary, during the act of clothing, but he must stand facing east when the Senior Warden addresses the Candidate.. After the Master's address he leads the Candidate to a point about two feet in front of the Master's pedestal. His only duties during the remainder of the ceremony are to ensure that the Candidate does not take a step before the signs which are demonstrated incidentally in the course of the narrative, but that he *does* take a step during the full explanation. The Candidate does *not* repeat any words at the latter point. Once the ceremony has been completed, he must not forget to take the Candidate to a seat in the Lodge, though there may be a short delay as the Master may well wish to congratulate him – and perhaps to present him with a ritual and a pair of gloves.

Chapter 7

Installation

In the ceremony of Installation the Senior Deacon has no duties to perform. There is, however, one point which deserves attention. When he is invested, he is entrusted with his wand. This he transfers momentarily to his left hand in order to shake hands with the Master. That done, he immediately transfers it back to his right hand, so that when he is conducted to his seat by the Installing Master (or Director of Ceremonies) the latter takes him by the right wrist or forearm. The wand should *not* be carried in the left hand at this point.

Appendix A

Checklist

1st Degree: –

2nd Degree: Ascertain correct starting point for
                  the steps
                  Location of Sq.

3rd Degree: Ascertain point for edge of s...t

Appendix B

The Immortal Memory...

For some people remembering words seems to be easy. Most of us find that it takes some effort. Older generations (including mine) had to learn poetry and passages of Shakespeare at school, and we probably did it – at least to start with – "parrot-fashion", that is, by rote. Educational methods have changed over the years and many younger readers will not have had that grounding. On the other hand, memorising things seems to get harder as we get older, so perhaps younger Brethren still have the advantage of those of us who have had more practice!

In a short appendix I cannot hope to do more than point out a few strategies that may help both older and younger readers in the task of memorising and recalling the words of the ritual. As a general observation, however, it cannot be stressed too much that no one who cannot render at least the sense of the words of the Ritual with reasonable fluency will be fully able to put across the ceremonies, and the important lessons they set out to teach, to a Candidate. A Master, or more junior Officer, who does not have to worry about getting more or less the right words out is able to concentrate on putting across their meaning and will, moreover, gain a great deal in confidence from the knowledge that he has the words at his command.

The most important thing is to allow plenty of time for the process of learning, and to have some appreciation of how long that process will take. No one who is not an expert in the techniques of memorising can hope to learn twenty pages of ritual to the required standard in, say, forty-eight hours.

Secondly, it is important to be familiar with and to understand what the words *mean* before starting to learn them. Without a feel for the shape of a passage of ritual, the message that is being conveyed and the key words and phrases, learning will be harder and will be a matter of learning the words parrot-fashion.

Thirdly, what fixes a passage in the memory is the effort of dragging it out again, rather than the mere repetition of the words. So it is important, when settling down with the book to do the hard work of learning, not to glance immediately at the book when a word or phrase proves elusive.

Fourthly, it is important not to bite off too much to learn at once. Some Brethren will try to learn a whole ceremony, or at least a sizeable chunk, as a single unit. It is not uncommon to hear a Brother who is delivering, say, the Charge after Initiation, start very well indeed, but deteriorate more and more rapidly as he progresses. The reason will almost certainly be that each time he has settled down to learn it he has started at the beginning and has advanced as far as time and his concentration have permitted, so that the early part of the passage is considerably more familiar than the later parts. A useful strategy, therefore, is to start some learning sessions in the middle of the passage or, better still, with the final paragraph, progressing to the last two paragraphs, then the last three, and so on. It is an interesting psychological fact that most listeners will rate a ceremony that starts and finishes well more highly than one that tails off badly towards the end, even if the latter is overall the more accurate ceremony.

Fifthly, "easy come, easy go". Something that is learnt quickly over a short period will be forgotten equally quickly unless steps are taken to fix it in the memory. Periodically running over a passage at regular, though increasing, intervals will help in this process.

Sixthly, the use of mnemonics can be extraordinarily helpful, and anyone can make up his own. Those with some familiarity with the history of the First World War will know of the nursing service, the Voluntary Aid Detachment (V.A.D.); this is a useful mnemonic for the Address to the Master in the Installation: "...

and by *virtuous*, *amiable* and *discreet* conduct...". In many ways, moreover, the more abstruse a mnemonic is the more likely it is to stick in the mind.

* * *

Not everything will work for everyone, but the following method of learning which I use myself when learning a new passage of ritual may be helpful to some readers of this book:

1. I spend about a fortnight making myself familiar with the shape and meaning of the passage I am learning. I try to read it over once a day, preferably last thing at night before I turn out the light, so that it is swirling around in my subconscious as I am dropping off to sleep.

2. Once I feel comfortable with the passage, I settle down with the book for the hard slog of learning. I find that there is, unfortunately, no substitute for this. I try to get through this stage as quickly as possible.

3. Next comes the first part of the process of fixing, by dragging the words back out of my memory. I try to do this with the book handy for the shortest time possible.

4. Once I feel reasonably confident of being able to recall the words, I make use of "dead" time (while I am walking, for example) when I cannot do anything else that is useful, to run over the passage in my mind. Because in those circumstances I cannot keep referring to the book, I find this part of the process particularly effective in getting the words firmly into my memory.

5. Once I think I know the passage, I keep repeating the previous step until the words become almost second nature. Only then am I really able to deliver the passage under "real" conditions. Unfortunately it is not always possible to have achieved this degree of polish before the passage has to be delivered.

6. Thereafter it is a matter of continuing to apply the polish. I am sometimes asked how long it has taken me to learn a particular piece of ritual; if the piece is the Seventh Section of the First Lecture, my reply is: one week – and over thirty years. I was much younger when I originally learnt it and I doubt if I could manage the initial stages so quickly today! But it is the polish that I have applied over the succeeding years that really matters.